BREEDING LOVEBIRDS

CONTENTS:

PHOTO CREDITS

Tony Silva: 10, 14, 18 (top), 19, 67, 71 (top), 78, 87 (bottom), 90; Barbara Kotlar: 15 (bottom), 70, 71 (bottom), 74, 75; Glen S. Axelrod: 6 (top), 18 (bottom), 20-21, 34-35, 38-39, 44, 49, 52, 53, 56, 58-59, 64, 65, 66; Dr. Herbert R. Axelrod: Front and back endpapers, title page, 8, 11, 12-13, 15 (top), 20 (top), 22, 23, 34 (top), 40, 41, 45 (top), 77, 79 (bottom), 80-81, 82, 83, 91; Dr. Matthew Vriends: 6-7, 87 (top); Harry V. Lacey: 9; A.J. Mobbs: 26; Kerry Donnelly: 16, 38 (top), 45 (bottom), 48, 93; Courtesy of Vogelpark Walsrode: 12 (top), 30, 37, 86; Courtesy of San Diego Zoo: 27 (bottom), 31, 79 (top); Miceli Studios: 60, 61.

ISBN 0-87666-831-7

Distributed in the U.S. by T.F.H. Publications, Inc., 211 West Sylvania Avenue, PO Box 427, Neptune, NJ 07753; in England by T.F.H. (Gt. Britain) Ltd., 13 Nutley Lane, Reigate, Surrey; in Canada to the pet trade by Rolf C. Hagen Ltd., 3225 Sartelon Street, Montreal 382, Quebec; in Southeast Asia by Y.W. Ong, 9 Lorong 36 Geylang, Singapore 14; in Australia and the South Pacific by Pet Imports Pty. Ltd., P.O. Box 149, Brookvale 2100, N.S.W. Australia; in South Africa by Valid Agencies, P.O. Box 51901, Randburg 2125 South Africa. Published by T.F.H. Publications, Inc., Ltd, the British Crown Colony of Hong Kong.

BREEDING LOVEBIRDS

**TONY SILVA
and
BARBARA KOTLAR**

Lovebirds are lively, active, pretty birds that are popular with both beginning and experienced bird keepers. **Below:** The Madagascar lovebird is one of the rarer and more expensive lovebirds.

Introduction

Lovebirds belong to the group *Agapornis*. They obtain the name "Lovebird" from the amount of mutual preening with which the birds occupy themselves. They are well-known birds and are popular all over the world. Since they breed readily in captivity, they are attractive to amateur as well as professional aviculturists. The lovebirds also freely hybridize so breeding them is a very interesting endeavor.

Lovebirds have attained great popularity because of their beauty, liveliness, and comical habits. They are short stocky birds with a large bill and a square or round tail.

2

Breeders have developed different color varieties of several lovebirds. Included among the species for which color varieties have been developed are the peach-faced (1) and the Nyasaland (2).

Common to them all is the green on their bodies with other variations of color. Although they can be noisy, they are still heavily in demand and can be found bred in aviaries in the United States and abroad. They are available in most pet shops and even dime stores.

There are many mutations of the peach-faced, Fischer's black-masked, Nyasaland, and even the red-faced. These mutations are available in blue, silver, albino, lutino, etc. There are nine species with five subspecies but four of the species are very similar and often treated as subspecies of a single species. Of these, all but the Swindern and its two subspecies are available, at least from time to time. The red-faced is rare but often obtainable at a high price.

Because most lovebirds will accept a regular nest box, except for the red-faced, which uses a termite mound, they are very desirable to breed. The purpose of this book is to acquaint the aviculturist with the breeding activities of the lovebird and to serve as a guide to the fascinating process of its reproduction.

1

It is often difficult to tell exactly what a baby bird will look like when it is mature. (1) This baby peach-faced lovebird will eventually become fully and colorfully feathered, and its beak will soon lighten in color. (2) This peach-faced displays the lighter beak and colorful appearance of a healthy adult.

2→

One of the most popular
and easiest to breed
lovebirds (once you are
sure that you have a true
pair) is the blue-masked.
Below: This is just one of
the several different ways
to set up breeding aviaries
and cages.

*Captive
Breeding*

The time has arrived for the aviculturist to begin to enthusiastically conserve wildlife. Many countries are prohibiting the export of all fauna. However, some species of birds are considered agricultural pests and as such are being persecuted. Some countries which prohibit such exports and claim to be highly protective of wildlife issue permits to shoot the birds, as is the case in Australia.

Since many countries have strict export regulations, the price and scarcity of birds are increased. Breeders can con-

1

(1) Abyssinian lovebirds are beautiful, quiet and not very aggressive. These two young cock Abyssinians were cage-bred by Ron Filip. (2) Unfortunately, there is a danger in keeping a group of black-masked lovebirds; adults are apt to feather pluck and in other ways injure youngsters. (3) Because of their aggressiveness, peach-faced lovebirds should be paired off and then each pair housed separately.

The comical antics of lovebirds help to endear them to their keeper. Such antics include the unusual positions a lovebird will assume in order to bathe itself.

tribute a wealth of knowledge and in some cases can help to establish and maintain species that are rare or endangered.

The role of the aviculturist has changed from merely keeping birds to breeding and conserving species. Certain pesticides whose use is regulated in the United States are freely used abroad. Land clearance is also a major threat to many species. Such land clearance and pesticides are deeply hurting the wild populations. Many blame aviculturists for the destruction of species because of demand for the pet market. This is not usually the case. Land clearance is the single greatest threat to the survival of any species. In the West Indies and in South America huge tracts of land are being cleared for agriculture and the raising of cattle. This has also occurred in Indonesia and Africa. Land is being cleared at a rapid rate. Such land or forest is never replaced, but is lost forever. The welfare of the people of a country is more important than the preservation of a species of bird, fish or any wild animal. Since this is the case, provision should be made so that these creatures are available to breeders interested in preserving the species. Often zoos do not have the resources or interest to do so. Most parrot breeding, for example, is being done by private individuals.

The time has come for aviculturists to play an important role and begin breeding birds. The beginning bird fancier can also lend his time and talent. Some birds once considered impossible to breed are being presently raised in large numbers. It has been proven that Mother Nature will work and help those who are trying to save a species. Some breeding programs have been extremely successful. Certain "endangered" birds can no longer be considered as such. Today, more knowledge is available about the care, food and breeding of birds than was true several years ago.

Lovebirds are ideal birds for a beginning breeder. They are hardy, very attractive, readily available, and in most cases prove to be good breeding stock. Some species, such as the black-cheeked lovebird, have very restricted ranges which helps make domestic breeding interesting and desirable. Lovebirds are relatively inexpensive so they can be easily afforded by the small breeder.

Some of the color mutations are expensive and very beautiful, and therefore, are more attractive for the breeder who is able to invest more money. However, not all lovebirds are to be called "beginner's birds," for some species prove difficult to breed and acclimate.

Those lovebirds which are handfed become rather tame. Most are kept in pairs for their beauty. Some become truly affectionate while others can become savage and mean without human contact.

It is the object of this book to introduce the different species of these birds to those who are admirers of lovebirds but most of all to interest individuals in captive breeding.

1

2

3

(1) These aviaries are used very successfully for lovebirds. Designed and built by Don Moss of Seffner, Florida, the aviaries are easy to clean. (2) Some bird keepers attach the nest box to the outside of the cage or aviary for easier access to the nest, while other keepers place the whole nest box in the aviary or cage. (3) Don Moss raised and hand-fed this lovebird.

Peach-faced lovebirds
are very easy to
breed in captivity.
Below: Breeding
operations may be
set up in outdoor
aviaries.

*Species
Of
Lovebirds*

PEACH-FACED LOVEBIRD *(Agapornis roseicollis)*

The males and females are alike. There is no sexual dimorphism. The birds have a green body with a blue rump. The beak is horn color and the face is rose; the feet are gray. The immatures are recognized by a dark black, strongly edged upper mandible. Some birds recently have had reddening of the feathers which in some cases disappears. Several birds with red are presently being bred in the hope that a spectacular red can be achieved. It seems to derive from a malnutrition problem or heredity.

1

There are a great many different color mutations of the peach-faced lovebird. (1) True albino peach-faceds should have red eyes and no pigment in their feathers, while lutino peach-faceds retain the peach tones and the rest of the body is intense yellow. (2) This is the golden-cherry mutation. (3) There are a variety of pied mutations of the peach-faced; this is a blue pied.

2   3

The peach-faced lovebird comes from Southwest Africa. Most of the birds offered for sale are captive raised. Rarely are the wild birds imported. These are the most commonly bred lovebirds and are presently available in a host of colors and mutations. All of the mutations are as hardy as the original bird, with the exception of the lutino, which is delicate until the first molt. These birds are found in open land, close to water, as well as on arid land. They are seen in flocks of approximately twenty birds. They feed on fruit, seeds and buds. When food is plentiful, they are observed in very large flocks.

Peach-faced lovebirds will freely nest in captivity and even hybridize. The greatest problem the breeder encounters with these birds is in obtaining a pair, not in having difficulty in actually breeding them. These birds will successfully breed in small cages. They will carry nesting material, such as newspaper and palm fronds, into the nest box. If palm fronds or willow branches are provided, the lovebirds will run a piece through their beaks several times to soften it. This is helpful in maintaining the high humidity needed by these birds for egg hatching.

The peach-faced lovebirds are highly pugnacious so it is recommended that they not be bred in a colony since pairs prove highly aggressive toward each other and chicks. They cannot be trusted with other birds or birds of their own kind because of their spiteful nature. They are probably the noisiest of all the lovebirds.

RED-FACED LOVEBIRD (Agapornis pullaria)

The male has a reddish orange bill and a red face. The rump is blue, the body green. The tail has a black band and red and green feathers. The feet are gray. The female has less red, actually tending toward orange. The head color varies from specimen to specimen. The best way to sex the birds is to observe that in the hen the underwing coverts are green while in the cock they are usually black. The immatures are like the adults but have less color. They tend to be more yellowish. The males have black wing coverts while the females lack this feature. This helps to distinguish the cocks from hens at an early age.

The red-faced lovebird has a large distribution in central Africa. It is found in lowland forests, highly timbered areas and cultivated areas.

In the wild this lovebird feeds on millets, seeds, fruits and buds of several trees. The red-faced lovebird must be fed on a shelf and not on a floor since it will not descend to the ground to feed. If not fed a proper diet, yellowing of the feathers will occur.

This bird is very difficult to breed since in the wild, termite mounds are used as nesting places. The mounds vary in color from brown to black and usually the tallest termite mounds created from trees are used. Feathers are sometimes added by the bird to the inside of the nesting area.

On several occasions the authors have observed that the bird has used a nest box which is very small and is made of cork or even peat. Cork can be glued together to form a square measuring a foot or less. The incubation period of the four or five eggs is approximately twenty-three days. To achieve success the box should be heated to a temperature of eighty-five degrees.

The red-faced lovebird enjoys most fruits and seeds and even mealworms and crickets from which the legs have been removed. It has proved to be a delicate bird and highly nervous. The few that have been imported generally command good prices.

ABYSSINIAN LOVEBIRD (Agapornis taranta)

The male has a red bill and a green body; there is red on its forehead. The wing flight feathers are black. The females lack the red on the forehead. Some aviculturists believe that the underwing coverts are black in males and

←**1**

2

(1) Red-faced lovebirds and (2) Swindern lovebirds are native to the continent of Africa, while (3) Madagascar lovebirds are found only on the island from which their name is taken.

3

27

green in hens. However, two females which the authors observed also showed some black. Immatures are similar to adults, but the males slowly develop red on the face. The beak is horn color with a black tip for the male as well as the female Abyssinian lovebird.

These very beautiful lovebirds originate in the highlands of Ethiopia. Small flocks of the birds are found in different kinds of forests. Fruit, wild seeds and figs are the staples of their diet.

These birds are infrequently available and are established in captivity or commonly bred. One breeder has recently produced ten specimens in two years. The female pulled out the cock's red head feathers before nesting, and occupied herself by throwing nesting material out of the nesting box instead of adding anything to it. The female appeared to be the more aggressive and dominant bird. They were bred in very small cages using small nest boxes. A double parakeet cage and a small budgie nest box can be utilized. These birds are calm and naturally gentler than most species.

MADAGASCAR LOVEBIRD *(Agapornis cana)*

The males have a gray head and upper breast with a green body. The bill is silver, and the feet are gray. The hens are all green with a horn color bill; the feet are gray. The immatures are similar to the adults.

These lovebirds come from the island of Madagascar where the export of birds, aquarium plants and fish is prohibited. The birds being imported to the United States come from Europe where they are aviary-raised. These sexually dimorphic lovebirds are very expensive. They are not commonly bred and are considered one of the rarer lovebirds.

SWINDERN LOVEBIRD *(Agapornis swinderniana)*

A very poorly known green bird with a blue rump. There

is a black collar at the back of the neck. The bill is dark. It is found in western Africa and the Congo but is rarely imported.

WHITE EYE-RING SPECIES

There are four lovebirds that are generally grouped by aviculturists under the catch-all name of "the white eye-ring species" for purposes of identification. Regardless of the coloration of the feathering of these birds and regardless also of their exact taxonomic placement, all have a comparatively large ring of white around their eyes; no other lovebird species has such a ring.

Authorities differ as to the taxonomic status of the birds involved. Some authorities (Forshaw in *Parrots of the World*, Walters in *The Complete Birds of the World*) consider them to be full species, whereas others regard them all as subspecies of *Agapornis personata*. We lean to the idea of treating them all as subspecies of one species. The four birds concerned are: *Agapornis personata fischeri*, Fischer's lovebird (given full specific status by Forshaw as *Agapornis fischeri*); *Agapornis personata personata*, the masked lovebird (*Agapornis personata* in Forshaw); *Agapornis personata lilianae*, the Lilian's or Nyasaland lovebird (*Agapornis lilianae* in Forshaw); and *Agapornis personata nigrigenis*, the black-cheeked lovebird (Forshaw's *Agapornis nigrigenis*).

Of the subspecies or species listed, two are common, while two are comparatively scarce but at least obtainable from time to time. One subspecies, *A. personata personata*, is available in two distinctly different colors. One, known generally as the black masked lovebird or black-masked lovebird, has a yellow chest and green wings and underparts to go with its black-masked head; the other, generally called either the blue-masked lovebird or the blue mutation of the masked lovebird, has the black masking over the head but has an over-all bluish coloration, with silvery white feathering at the throat.

1

There are four white eye-ring species: (1) Fischer's lovebird, (2) Nyasaland or Lilian's lovebird, (3) black-cheeked lovebird, and the commonly found black-masked lovebird.

2

3

You can easily see how the niceties of language (especially printed language) can play a big part in the formation of common names of birds; the presence or absence of a hyphen in a printed name, for example, can cause consternation. The common name of *Agapornis personata personata,* for instance, often is rendered as "black-masked lovebird," the meaning of which to the uninitiated but literate reader of bird lore would mean that *Agapornis personata personata* is a lovebird having a black mask. (Let us leave aside for the moment the question of whether "mask" in this instance is the right word to use or whether "capped" or "hooded" or "headed" would be more proper.) Yet the same bird is often called in print "black masked lovebird." The absence of the hyphen in this case would lead the normal reader to believe that the bird is generally black (or at least dark) in general coloration and that it possesses a mask of some type. The reader would conclude also that the mask is of some color or shade other than black, because if it weren't it wouldn't show at all against the unrelieved darkness of the bird.

When the blue mutation of *Agapornis personata personata* is taken into consideration the problem becomes even more severe, because here the situation is exactly the opposite. You *can't* use a hyphen to denote the masked condition of the bird, even though it is indeed masked (or hooded or capped or whatever other word you've chosen to denote the condition of having the head covered in black). This bird is most properly described as the "blue masked lovebird"—it's blue, and it has a mask. If you were to call it the blue-masked lovebird, you'd be saying that it is a lovebird with a blue mask, and that is not so.

BLACK-MASKED LOVEBIRD *(Agapornis personata personata)*

The body of this lovebird is green with a yellow upper breast and black face. It has a red bill and brown feet. The immatures are similar to the adults except that the young specimens have black toward the tip of the bill.

FISCHER'S LOVEBIRD (*Agapornis personata fischeri*)

The head and upper breast of this lovebird are an orange-red. The bill is red and the body green. It has gray-brown feet. The immatures also have dark on their bill.

BLACK-CHEEKED LOVEBIRD (*Agapornis personata nigrigenis*)

The top of the head is brownish, with black areas only below the eyes. There is a reddish patch on the throat. By being restricted to Zambia and vicinity, this lovebird has the smallest range of any lovebird.

LILIAN'S OR NYASALAND LOVEBIRD (*Agapornis personata lilianae*)

Even though this bird is similar to Fischer's, there are several features which distinguish it. The Fischer's rump is blue and larger than that of the Nyasaland which has a smaller green rump. The bird has an orange-red head and has a red bill like all other white eye-ring species. The body is green and the feet are gray-brown.

The range of the white eye-ring species is Tanzania and Zambia. It is found in wooded areas, semi-forest, and cultivated land. In captivity the black-masked and Fischer's are found to be the subspecies most commonly being bred. Many breeders feel that the Fischer's fare best in a two-pair colony. In the wild these birds feed on cultivated grains, wild seeds, seeding grass and grains.

Albino lovebirds command a high price because they are not very common. **Below:** One way to increase the availability of those lovebirds not found commonly is to increase the number of commercial breeding operations.

Availability

Availability of a species depends on several factors: import and export regulations, desirability of the bird for the breeder, and actual number in existence. The most commonly available lovebirds are as follows:

Peach-faced lovebird
Black-masked lovebird
Fischer's lovebird.

The above listed are almost always on the market. Several colors or mutations are also available. Some of these mutations include pied, blue peach-face, and blue black-masked.

Those lovebirds which are sometimes obtainable but costly and generally sought after only by advanced hobbyists are:

Black-cheeked lovebird

Nyasaland lovebird

Madagascar lovebird

Abyssinian lovebird.

Those which are not available or when captured rarely survive are the following:

Red-faced lovebird

Swindern lovebird.

Lovebirds come from two sources—those caught in the wild and those bred in aviaries either in the United States or abroad. Cockatiels are being raised commercially in great numbers in Africa and in some aviaries in Brazil. Lovebirds are also being bred on a large scale. Some breeders use huge flights for the birds being bred in the colony system. This does not always prove a good method, as it affords no way to control matings and breeding. Generally, if birds are raised commercially, numerous pairs with many nesting boxes are introduced and allowed to breed indiscriminately with each other. More exacting breeders house two or three pairs to a flight and control the matings.

The number of birds actually removed from their natural habitat is small when considering the breeding potential of a flock. Some governments regulate the number caught and sold. In the country of Guyana approximately 15 thousand birds were exported in 1979. This is quite a small number since the bird population in Guyana is estimated to be about seven hundred thousand.

The birds are generally held in cages until export. Orders are then received and shipments sent by freight. Some birds, such as cockatoos, are sometimes shipped one to a compartment in a shipping crate. However, lovebirds are usually shipped in crates which can contain many birds.

Imported birds caught in the wild are placed in quarantine for thirty days upon arrival in this country. Here they

Breeding Abyssinian lovebirds is made a bit easier because the sexes can be easily distinguished; the male has a red patch on his forehead.

are fed a medicated mash that contains chlorotetracycline or CTC for ornithosis and are checked for Newcastle disease. Birds proven to have Newcastle are either destroyed or sent to a country that will accept them. Birds are sometimes fed boiled cracked maize before being exported.

Often several thousand lovebirds are in quarantine at one time. All of these birds are banded, which is required by law for all imported birds. It is difficult to imagine employees undertaking this task!

After being checked, found healthy and released by the Department of Agriculture, the birds are sold either to pet shops or to wholesale distributors.

One lovebird kept as a pet does not require a band. **Below:** Many lovebirds kept for breeding purposes must be banded if pairs and chicks are to be distinguished.

General Maintenance

RECORD KEEPING

All lovebirds bred by the aviculturist should be banded. The bands are sold locally or can be obtained from the ALS (American Lovebird Society). Such bands are very helpful in keeping track of the chicks and parents.

The breeder should make every effort to keep good, clear records of matings and hatchings when breeding birds of any species. Such records will be very beneficial. The information can be utilized when setting up new pairs of birds. It is also a guide as to precisely which birds have been rested so overbreeding will not occur. A small card should be attached directly to the nest box for data to be recorded. More extensive records can be kept in a notebook. The card attached to the nest box should supply the dates of breeding, the date of eggs laid, the pair band numbers and

Banding would best be handled by two people; (1) one person holds the bird and the other slides on the band. (2) The band should be slid over the front toes with the rear toes folding back. (3) Make sure the rear toes can be clearly seen; otherwise, one might be torn off.

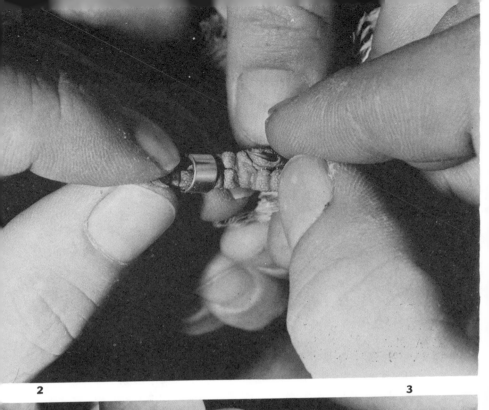

2

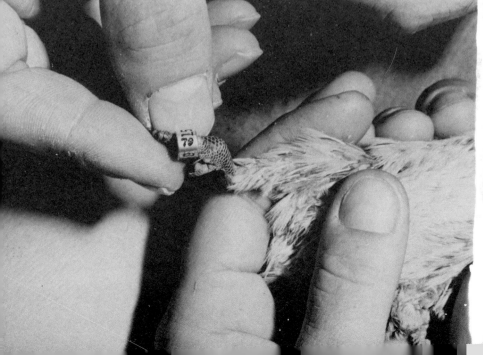

3

the number of eggs hatched and unhatched. Ideally the cage should be assigned a record number for ease of recognition if several or many cages are used.

A studbook can be kept by those bird fanciers breeding rare or endangered species. Presently there is a studbook for endangered Amazons. It offers information about the species, to prevent inbreeding.

At the present time all birds coming through quarantine are being banded. No two importers are assigned the same number to avoid confusion when the birds are used for breeding or are being sold.

CAGING

There is a variety of cages being offered to the breeder to house lovebirds. Many lovebirds are being kept and bred successfully in cages. A larger size cage is more desirable since the birds can exercise; however, the authors have observed pairs of peach-faced being bred in small cages on shelves in pet shops. These cages measure two feet square. A cage which is three feet square is more desirable since the birds are thus less confined.

The cage should be placed off the floor to avoid drafts and even the mice that find the seed in the feeding dishes very attractive. Placing the cage on a table or even hanging it from the ceiling alleviates these problems. It is also easier to keep the area clean if one can sweep under the cage. The cage should be placed in a spot in sunlight or artificial light. A ventilated area is ideal, but it must be draft-free. If hanging more than one cage, a space of at least two inches between them is necessary to prevent the toes being bitten by birds in the adjoining cage. Perches in the cage should be positioned at opposite ends of the cage so as to not prevent the birds from flying. One perch should be placed high up; on it roosting can take place.

Flights are preferred by many breeders if there is sufficient room since the lovebirds do not have to be moved after being bred. However, if there is a colony of lovebirds in one flight, fights can break out between breeding pairs over roosting spots. It is not unusual for pairs of parrots to want the same nest box. More time and energy is spent squabbling over territory than in actual breeding. It would be desirable if each breeding pair could have its own flight.

An outdoor flight is very suitable for warm climates. It must be constructed well so the birds cannot escape and rodents cannot enter. The mesh used should be small enough so the birds won't become caught in it. A concrete floor in the flight makes cleaning easy since it can be hosed down daily. Part of the flight should be covered to provide shade and protection from rain. The flights can be any size, depending on available space. Ideal flights measure eight to ten feet long, six feet high, and three or four feet wide.

One type of flight that is highly recommended and very effective is that used by Life Fellowship in Tampa, Florida. This is designed to raise endangered Amazon parrots. The flights are hung several feet from the floor and have a mesh bottom. Ramon Noegel, director of the ranch, feels there is less risk of the birds developing worms from eating spoiled food, droppings, etc. The debris falls through the bottom of the cage. The birds remain quite calm since it is not necessary to enter the flight for cleaning.

Indoor flights can be built with the same idea in mind but somewhat different in construction. Messrs. Ken Schulz and Fred Frencl , successful lovebird breeders, use flights four feet long, two feet wide, and two feet high. They hang them and use a mesh bottom. Several perches of different sizes are available as well as an area for free flight.

An absorbent material should be used on the bottom of a cage or a flight. Newspaper is the cheapest but it must be changed daily. Ground corn cobs and pine or cedar shavings are other suitable choices for the bottom of the cage. They are highly absorbent and require only weekly cleaning depending upon the number of birds. If no material is

Lovebirds may be bred in cages and aviaries of various sizes. (1) Some bird keepers house individual pairs of birds in individual cages. (2) Other keepers breed birds in large, uniformly constructed aviaries. (3) Other breeders use a combination of cages and aviaries.

2

3

used in the cage, the droppings and food debris can be scraped often and wiped or swept away.

A light should be used above or in the cage or flight. An especially good facsimile for sunlight is a Vita Lite. However, wires should not be exposed, for the birds may chew them. Conduit will protect the wires from being bitten.

If a flight is used, it should contain a slot for a feeding tray. Food, water, oyster shell, etc. are placed on this. Thus, flights do not have to be entered for feeding and watering.

FEEDING

Through proper feeding most birds can be encouraged to breed. Diet is a very important factor in breeding lovebirds or any other birds. Lovebirds need a balanced yet varied diet to maintain proper health and vigor.

Variety is the spice of life even for birds. Many table scraps could be fed to most birds without harm. These should not be greasy or spicy. Some breeders feed boiled chicken which is consumed by many other species of birds too, not only parrots. Vegetables can safely be offered and often are relished by many species. Boiled rice with an addition such as egg is consumed readily by many parrot-type birds. Boiled rice is used in some Asian countries for hand-feeding cockatoos. Sometimes it is ground, or the birds are taught to eat it directly from bowls. Many pet parrots will pick at the bones of chicken for small pieces of meat. Pet birds, when offered the bone of a drumstick, will enjoy many hours of pleasure. Within reason, one must offer the birds what they like. This is what Ramon Noegel believes. His success with Amazons, considered one of the most difficult parrots to breed, has been unprecedented. The key to healthy birds is a varied diet of many cooked foods as well as items not ordinarily fed to parrots or birds. He also feeds several mixes which are consumed eagerly by his parrots.

An exclusively seed diet may not prove adequate or sufficiently nutritional for birds. Some species will also consume nectar. Others feed on fruit and certain seeds of grass or millets, while others feed on hard palm nuts. Birds have different tastes just as humans do. Some crave certain foods, while others dislike a particular offering.

Food should be available at all times; the absence of it could prove fatal. If a bird owner goes on vacation, he should make arrangements for someone to feed his birds. Even if it is only seeds, it is necessary to keep food and water always available for the bird. This is of particular importance when chicks are being raised. Food is continually in demand by the ever-hungry chicks. Often birds have to be boarded by a veterinarian or special kennel that accepts birds when the aviculturist finds it necessary to be away.

FRUITS AND VEGETABLES

A few lovebirds will eat large quantities of fruit. Usually, though, only small amounts will be consumed; however, fruits and vegetables should be included in all birds' diets. Because they are easily digested and bulky, many birds will feed on greater amounts while rearing chicks. Fruits and vegetables provide many vitamins, minerals, and enzymes needed by birds. Approximately one-third of the daily food allocation to the authors' birds consists of fruits and vegetables. Some vegetables have a high vitamin A content which is needed in great amounts by some species of birds, especially the eclectus parrots. The absence of vitamin A in the diet invites the development of the fungus called "candida", which could prove to be fatal.

Many birds will at first consume little fruits or vegetables. If fed to them every day, the birds will gradually sample them. Placing birds which are good and adventuresome eaters with more finicky birds will prove worthwhile. If they refuse the fresh produce, do not give up but keep offering it to them. They will slowly start sampling

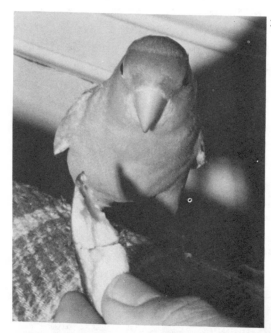

Some lovebirds become so tame that they will take food from their owners' hands. (1) Fruits, (2) seeds and (3) vegetables should all be included in a lovebird's diet.

3

and eating them. Lovebirds will eat small amounts of apples and a variety of vegetables and other fruits. Once the birds begin eating them, vitamins and minerals can be sprinkled on the fruits and vegetables. Wheat germ or cod liver oil, which is high in vitamins E and A, should also be added. All fruits and vegetables should be chopped fine, with a few exceptions. Carrots and endive finely chopped or even offered whole are very popular with birds.

SEEDS

A seed diet should include a variety of items. The choice varies from breeder to breeder. About two-thirds of a bird's diet should consist of seeds and one-third should be fruit, vegetables, egg foods and mixes.

Recently there has been a change from seeds to pellets which are manufactured by several firms in the country. These replace seeds in some places. One quarantine station is feeding a pellet diet to all the birds it handles. The pellets are medicated to follow guidelines for ornithosis or "parrot fever." They are red since it has been claimed that birds are attracted to that color. When the birds are first introduced to the quarantine station, they are fed a mixture of seeds and pellets. Then they are put on a diet of pellets. After they are released, they are switched back to seeds. It should be noted that the birds' droppings are red.

Seed should be fresh. It can easily be tested for freshness. The seed is soaked for twenty-four hours and then placed on a towel and kept moist. Fresh seed will soon sprout and it is especially high in protein when it begins to sprout. It should be checked regularly for moths. Insect-ridden seed is usually old or stale. However, moths often do get into fresh seed and are eagerly consumed by parrot-type birds. Occasionally check for dusty seeds and remove them. During the summer the seed should be purchased in small amounts, since fresh seed is the best. Store it in a cool, dry place.

Many breeders will re-use seeds offered to some picky birds. This idea is employed by Kenneth Schulz and Fred Frencl of Brookfield Aviaries. They daily offer fresh seeds to birds that are breeding. Those that are not breeding are fed the leftovers or the seed from another cage. This is one way to save money. Sometimes a bit of fresh seed is added. There is much waste in seeds, and even that which has been used a second time can serve as a food to outdoor wildlife. This economical method is being used with great success with small birds.

If the birds are kept outdoors, the seeds should be protected and placed away from direct sunlight and moisture. In addition to the seeds, the birds will also appreciate fresh twigs from which small amounts of bark will be consumed. Many truly enjoy feeding on bark, twigs and logs. However, be careful not to use anything that is poisonous.

Birds in the authors' possession are fed on sunflower seed, hemp, safflower, parakeet mix and thistle. Many aviculturists are eliminating sunflower seed because they claim that birds fed on it become lethargic and have little feather gloss, etc. Safflower seed, similar to sunflower seed but white and much smaller, is being used by many breeders to replace sunflower seed. It is said to help plumage, make the birds more active, and make them breed better. However, sunflower seed is still being fed successfully to many birds, even to those in very productive collections.

A mix that is commonly used for feeding lovebirds is as follows:

    1 part sunflower seed
    1 part safflower seed
    1 part parakeet mix.

To this, small amounts of the following can be added:

    hemp
    oats
    thistle.

1

2

3

(1) This mineral block has been well worn by a group of lovebirds. (2) Lovebirds should be provided with a variety of seeds, and (3) they occasionally enjoy millet sprays.

The seeds can be mixed, but some breeders prefer to feed them separately. Cod liver oil should not be sprinkled on seed since it rapidly becomes rancid.

A regular daily feeding can be as follows:

Morning: Eggs, corn on the cob, fruit and mixes. Most birds can be attracted to eating fruit at this time since they are very active in the morning.

Noon: Seed and fresh water with vitamins added.

Evening: Several peanuts, dog food, and raw vegetables.

There is less waste when there are several feedings. Other ingredients can also be added at each meal. This is the time seed bowls and water dishes should be checked. Frequency of feedings is one reason why many birds become very tame. The birds will anticipate the feeding and eagerly await the breeder's arrival. Contact with the birds several times daily helps the aviculturist form a relationship with his birds.

BUGIMINE OR PETAMIN

These foods are fed easily to the hungry chicks. They are made especially for adults with chicks in the nest. The birds will eat large quantities. A small dish of Bugimine or Petamin should always be available to birds rearing chicks. Birds being brought into breeding condition will also benefit greatly from them.

CUTTLEFISH BONE

This is torn to pieces by most larger parrot-type birds, but most species of lovebirds will make good use of cuttlefish bone too. It is rich in minerals and should be fed even in small quantities. Since cuttle bone is an excellent source of calcium, it is very important when chicks are in the nest. If calcium is not included in the diet, birds could develop rickets or softening of bones. Such conditions are rarely cured, and birds which suffer mild cases will have bowed legs. It is of prime importance that all birds be fed calcium, either in the form of calcium lactate or powder of cuttle bones. When raising chicks in an aviary, calcium should be added to the feed mix.

SALT LICK OR SALT BLOCK

This is made for rabbits but is relished by cockatiels and many other parrots. It serves as a source of iodine, and small amounts should be consumed by most birds. A salt lick can be hung very easily from the side of the cage. Parrots will pick and lick small quantities off the block.

GRAVEL OR GRIT

It is believed that because parrots have no teeth, gravel, grit or oyster shell is needed to help grind seeds in the crop. The oyster shell is preferred because it will disintegrate slowly and will remain in the crop for awhile. It is very important that these substances be available to birds, especially while breeding. Birds that are beginning to lay will consume great quantities. Oyster shell contains large amounts of calcium which helps in the formation of the egg shell. Offer a small bowl or dish to the birds at all times, and they will consume as much as needed.

BREADS AND CEREALS

Whole wheat bread, soaked in either water or milk, is readily accepted by most birds and is very high in protein. It can also be given dry or crumbled with cheese. Wheat bread is beneficial to adults in rearing chicks because it is bulky. It can be hung from the side of the cage to allow the bird to eat when it wishes. Cereal with preservatives and sugar can also be fed dry or soaked in milk or water.

MIXES

Mixes consist of many ingredients, both dry and liquid. A blender will come in handy in preparing a mix. Juices, such as carrot or beet, are usually the basis of a mix. To

Instead of using heavy food dishes in an aviary, some aviculturists use feeding stations which are off the ground (this discourages vermin) and which protect the food (from the birds' droppings).

this, wheat bread, peanuts, wheat germ, cereal, vitamins and minerals can be added. Softened unflavored gelatin can be blended in and the entire mixture should be warmed slowly but not brought to a boil. The birds will enjoy and consume the cooled mixture with great gusto. Cheese can also be added to form a crumbly mixture. This is a high protein mix and very beneficial to birds with chicks in the nest.

EGGS

Many breeders feed eggs to birds; however, fresh eggs should be fed in the morning since they spoil quickly, and any remains should be removed from the cage. Birds enjoy pecking on eggs that have been hard-boiled although some prefer them scrambled. If chicks are in the nest, eggs should be offered several times daily. All cups in which the eggs are placed should be cleaned and washed thoroughly. Bread crumbs, grated carrots, hulled sunflower seeds, and powdered milk can be added to the eggs.

WATER

Fresh water should be provided at least once a day. The feed and water dishes should be cleaned and washed with a mild soap or disinfectant and rinsed well daily. If placed in the heat and sun, a dish will develop a green algae growth. It will become slimy and bacteria will begin to grow if it is not kept clean. Vitamins should be added to the water daily.

FOOD DISHES

Breeders use ceramic, glass, plastic and metal dishes for water and food. The plastic ones must be heavy, or the birds will chew on them. If ceramic bowls are used, check that no poisonous glazes have been used in the firing of them. Glass, ceramic and metal all have the advantage of being kept clean and disinfected in the dish washer.

Once you know that you have a true pair, you can house them in a single cage that has an attached nest box. **Below:** Some aviculturists house several birds in an aviary and allow the birds to choose their own mates.

Breeding Lovebirds

SEXING

One of the greatest problems a breeder encounters is obtaining a true pair of lovebirds in a species which shows no sexual dimorphism, that is, no difference of form or color between members of the species. It is not unusual for two males to act like a pair and mate. Often two hens will lay eggs and incubate as a pair. When this happens, the clutches are even larger than average. The only accurate ways of procuring a true pair are to purchase a proven pair or to allow several lovebirds to choose mates and actually lay fertile eggs.

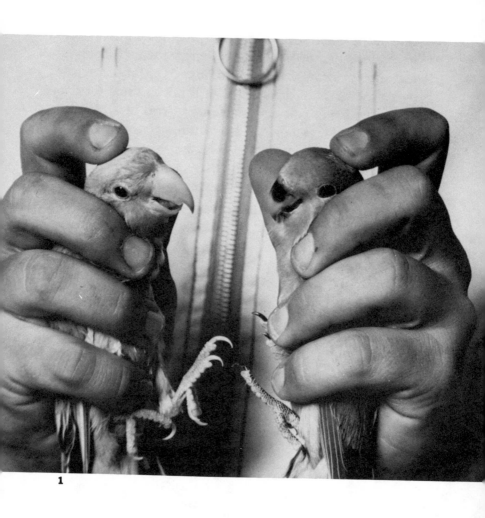

1

It usually is much easier to distinguish
between a young bird and an old one
than to determine the sex of a bird. (1) A
young peach-faced lovebird has a darker
bill than an adult and has no rose on its
head. (2) One method of determining sex
is to examine the bird's pelvic bones;
generally, females have a wider space
between the bones than do males.

2

61

2

(1) A nest box is actually very easy to construct if you have the wood and the right tools. (2) This is an inside view of a nest box.

The best way to obtain a pair is to purchase a half dozen lovebirds; through natural choice, a pair will emerge. Of course, this can be a very costly or even impossible method if space is a consideration. The two lovebirds which seek to become a pair will stake out a small territory and defend it with all their power. This area might well be a perch and the lovebirds will guard it from any intruders. Since lovebirds have a naturally aggressive personality, there can be quite a commotion in the cage when several birds are present. Care must be taken that a bird is not injured. It is impossible to maintain a group or colony of lovebirds for a length of time since they have such forceful dispositions. Often the introduction of a nest box will trigger breeding interest and the choosing of a mate. Some breeders believe natural pairing is the best way to obtain a good pair and they even use the method in species which are sexually dimorphic. Natural pairing is undoubtedly the best since mates of choice are obtained and natural pair bonds established.

It must not be assumed that just because a pair produces infertile eggs that they are two hens. Some "true" pairs can lay infertile eggs the first or even second try. Another misconception in the study of observing the sex of birds is that males will feed only females. This is not always the case with lovebirds and other parrot-type birds. Some hens may feed the cocks to attract attention. Males do not necessarily hold their tail feathers tight or closed to show their aggressiveness. Finally, it is not always true that hens have smaller heads and beaks while males have larger heads and slimmer beaks.

Often examining the pelvic bones might prove a worthwhile method of sexing lovebirds if the birds are in breeding condition. The pelvic bones are small bones located above the vent opening. In the cock these bones are very close together, almost touching, while in the hen they are further apart, thus allowing room for the egg to pass.

When the pelvic bone examination method is used, the birds should be held in a natural, straight stand-up or copulation position.

It is interesting to note that the hens will carry nesting material to the box on their bodies, usually the rump. An activity such as this should be observed and noted since it might provide information useful for future breedings.

BREEDING

Before lovebirds are bred, they should be in good health. When not being bred, the birds can be flighted to insure the proper exercise that is necessary for their well-being. Birds that have been flighted will generally prove very willing to nest, once a box is offered. The birds should never be overbred since their health and the quality of chicks might suffer. When overbred by inconsiderate breeders, the resistance of the birds is lowered, and they become weaker. Breeders should breed only the best quality available. Birds can be bred three times a year and then should be flighted or rested for the remainder of the time.

Lovebirds, like cockatiels, should be bred at no earlier than a year of age. They become sexually mature at twelve months. Some breeders wait until the birds are in their second year before they are bred.

Most lovebirds mate by the male stepping on the hen's back. She has her wings open to maintain balance. He will also open his wings for balance. The hen crouches down, and the mating takes place. The male's tail is placed on the side, and the vents touch. At this time sperm is transferred to the hen. Mating generally takes place in the morning or late afternoon although it can happen anytime. The birds might mate frequently or infrequently, depending on the pairs.

When a pair of birds is ready to begin breeding, the hen spends considerable time in the nesting box during the day and night. Her droppings will become larger and foul-

2

(1) This planted outdoor aviary provides protection from the elements. (2) Here the nest boxes are hung on the outside for easy inspection of chicks and eggs. Water bottles also attached to the outside are easily removed for filling and cleaning.

←1

smelling since hormones have been secreted in them. She will wait until she leaves the nesting box to excrete the droppings. The cock bird will begin feeding the hen. A swelling will appear in or near her vent. This is an egg which is being brought close to the vent for laying. The breeder should watch carefully at this point to make sure that all goes well.

As soon as the first egg is laid, the date is marked on the egg with a felt-tipped pen. This is more accurate than keeping track of the eggs on a piece of paper. The hen will begin incubating immediately. The embryo can easily be noticed in seven days. When the egg is placed on a small pen flashlight, small red veins can be seen. These are blood vessels, the sign of life.

If the first egg is infertile, it is generally the last if the birds do not mate often. It is best to leave an infertile egg with the hen so chicks won't develop spraddle legs. Even though the first clutch proves infertile, allow the pair to breed at least twice more before concluding the birds are not an actual pair.

The lovebird's incubation period is between twenty-two to twenty-four days, twenty-four being most accurate. Time will not differ between birds in the wild and those in captivity. Some breeders feel that how light the hen sits affects the incubation period.

The chicks will cut through the shell and free themselves by using their egg tooth. If a peeping chick does not hatch in thirty-six hours after it is heard, it generally dies. The chicks are quite normally tired and weak and need their first food supplied almost immediately by the hen. The egg tooth will fall out by itself.

Often hens and cocks will pluck their chick's head, wings, and back. These chicks will feather out once they are removed from the parents. When chicks are handfed, they feather out quickly. Lovebirds become independent in six to eight weeks.

The chicks should be banded with aluminum bands made especially for lovebirds. These can be purchased from an aviary supply house, bird clubs and some pet shops.

Nest inspection is common practice among aviculturists. It generally does not disturb the birds. This is important since it can reveal problems. The breeder can observe on a daily basis how the chicks are growing and can use this information for future nesting.

NESTING

The greatest problem a breeder will face in breeding lovebirds is getting the eggs to hatch. Many breeders find large numbers of chicks dead in the shell. These eggs cannot be hatched because the humidity is not high enough. Lovebirds need very high humidity for hatching. In the wild many use palm fronds in the nest. Such fronds have been softened by the bird by running them through its beak. This releases water which helps to maintain high humidity.

The dead-in-the-shell problem can be remedied several ways. The use of a humidifer or vaporizer helps maintain humidity of approximately sixty-five percent. The nest and eggs can be sprayed several times daily with water. Finally, a specially constructed box for nesting can be utilized.

Many breeders with only one or two cages choose not to go to the expense of buying a large humidifer. A vaporizer will serve the same purpose and is very easy to keep clean. This is a must since bacteria should not be permitted to grow. These appliances should not be allowed to run dry. Watch carefully to make sure that a humidity of sixty-five percent is reached.

The spraying of eggs is a common practice with parrot breeders. In the wild, rain finds its way into the nesting cavities used by parrots. A fine mist in a sprayer can be directed onto the birds and eggs. Some breeders will spray the nests twice a day and several times weekly when eggs

1

(1)This is a specially designed nest box. The bottle has holes drilled through the top which correspond to those holes on the bottom of the nest box. When filled with water, the bottle helps maintain the proper humidity inside the nest box. (2) Abyssinian or black-winged lovebirds can be aggressive toward their own kind—and other birds; they should not be colony bred. (3) Fischer's lovebirds and cockatiels are two commonly bred parrot species; here a Fischer's egg is next to a cockatiel's egg.

2

3

are nearing the hatching date. Spraying heavily the sides of the nesting box and nesting material will also prove effective.

A special nest box can be constructed to insure efficiency in maintaining high humidity. The box is made for most species of lovebirds; however, a few species prefer smaller boxes. The box measures six inches wide, eight inches long, and eight inches high. If too large a box is provided, the birds will stuff it with nesting material, thereby reducing its size considerably. Many lovebirds enjoy nesting in very restricted places.

A hole large enough for the bird to enter easily should be cut in the box. An outside perch placed just under the hole will facilitate easy entry and exiting. Several small holes should be drilled in the bottom of the box. A glass jar whose lid should also have the same number and size of holes should be aligned with the bottom of the box. The jar should be filled with water. This adds humidity to the nesting box.

A differently designed box which also proves an effective nesting ground for lovebirds is one that is slightly higher. A shallow tray to hold water is situated on the bottom of the box. A piece of fine mesh is secured above the tray and nailed to the walls of the nesting box. Shavings or other nesting materials are then added. The water provides proper humidity. The disadvantage of this set-up is that the nesting within the box has to be disturbed if more water needs to be added. However, a drawer arrangement can be incorporated in this box which facilitates refilling. Small holes should be drilled in both types of boxes to provide circulation of air.

Nesting materials generally used are pine shavings and peat moss or plain pine shavings. Peat moss which should be soaked for several days and then squeezed thoroughly serves quite adequately as a nesting material. It is then placed in the bottom of a cage with the shavings over it.

Several inches of nesting material should be provided so the bird can sort out what it desires. Paper and feathers are sometimes added by the lovebird to its nest.

The nesting box should be hung on the outside of the cage for easy inspection of the eggs, chicks and material. A small door is necessary so that the breeder can check the activities within the box. It should be attached as high as possible to the cage since birds feel more secure in a high nesting place. A perch should be positioned directly across from the entrance to the box to allow the lovebirds to fly freely in and out of the box. Most species of lovebirds will tolerate inspection of the box; however, sometimes a pair will become quite nervous at such action. If this is the case, it is best not to disturb them.

HANDFEEDING

Handfeeding or handrearing is a very old and successful method and results in very tame birds. This technique has been employed by Caribbean, Mexican, and Central and South American Indians for hundreds of years. Because the chicks are removed and fed by hand, they come to rely solely on people for their survival. This is beneficial for the breeder, chicks and parents.

The main reason for handfeeding lovebirds is to produce the tamest birds possible. The chicks become more docile and affectionate and relate to humans without fear. Handfed chicks are even less aggressive than very young birds that have been tamed. The parents might also nest a second time if the chicks are removed. This is very desirable if the birds are listed among the rare or endangered species. Some parrots might kill their chicks and raise only one, as is the case with cockatoos. Therefore, more chicks can be raised by the breeder if he employs the handfeeding method.

Most breeders remove the chicks two to three weeks after they hatch or just before the pin feathers begin to show. At this age they will readily accept food from people as well as

1

(1) Closed bands such as the one on this budgie chick help the breeder maintain proper records. Tools which could be used for hand-rearing parrot chicks include (2) an eyedropper and (3) a spoon.

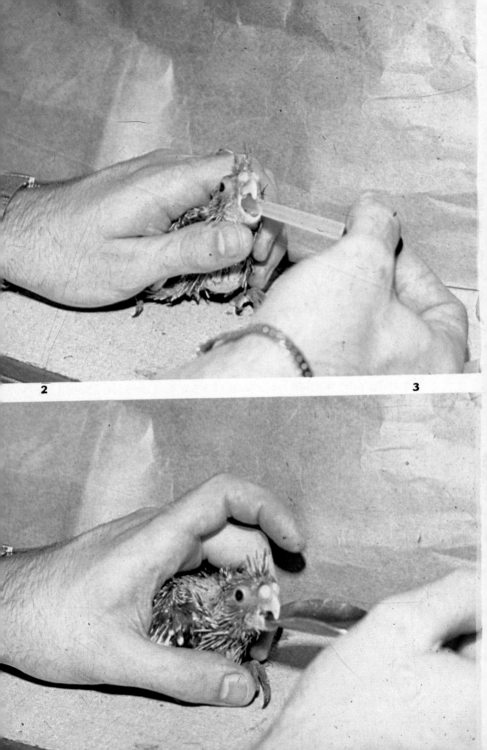

from their parents. The chicks should be placed in a nest box with shavings on the bottom. They should all be removed at one time since they will thus keep each other warm with their body heat. The nest box should be covered and placed in a warm spot.

When first removed from the parents, the chicks should be fed 4 times daily. If weight is not lost but is slowly gained, feedings should then proceed to 2-3 times daily. The following food formula can be used for the feeding.

One part sunflower seed hulled and without any shell. All stones and foreign matter must be removed. Grind the seed into a powder in a blender.

One part Purina Hi-Protein Monkey Chow. This must also be pulverized.

One-half part Hi-Protein baby cereal.

Mix together thoroughly in a small bowl and add some baby food vegetables such as spinach or carrots. A bit of scraped cuttlefish bone can also be added. Enough for one feeding only should be mixed at a time. The food should be kept warm, but not hot. Many chicks will refuse the food if it is cold or even cool.

An eye dropper can be used to handfeed the chicks. The tip should be cut on a slant to expedite feeding. Some breeders use a small spoon, such as a souvenir type with the edges bent upward for feeding. This is easier to keep clean than the eye dropper, but both are equally satisfactory.

The bird is held in one hand and the food fed with the other until the crop is slightly bulging. It is important that the last feeding of the day be late at night so that food is in the crop before retiring. As the chick gets older, the food offered should become thicker although more will be consumed.

After the chicks feather out, they should be placed either in a cage or fishtank, and seeds such as parakeet mix and sunflower should be provided on the bottom. Seed can also be placed in a seed cup. Water in a cup should be provided.

Both of these chicks are peach-faced lovebirds; the lighter one is twelve days old.

As the chicks mature, they can be checked regularly to be sure they are being properly nourished. It is natural for birds to consume less as they begin to fly. This is nature's way of getting them off the ground.

An impacted crop can be rectified by giving the chick liquids or saline water and kneading the food in the crop until it is slowly digested. Do not feed more solids, but give water mixed with a small amount of milk of magnesia. The droppings should be observed carefully to be sure they are normal and that the food is being digested. The authors once had a rare species of bird that had a slightly impacted crop. The chick was placed in an incubator and fed honey water for twenty-four hours. The food was slowly digested, and the chick survived. Small amounts of food were then given to the bird to prevent a repetition of the problem.

1

(1) This hand-reared Fischer's chick is learning to eat soft foods from a bowl. (2) These young black-masked lovebirds will soon be leaving the nest. (3) Here, young peach-faced lovebirds which have already left the nest are perching with their parents.

2

3

Providing a safe environment is only one of the responsibilities of a bird keeper. **Below:** The keeper must be sure that any plants provided for his birds have not been treated with chemicals and are not poisonous.

Diseases

The main concern of this book is breeding lovebirds. There are on the market several excellent books which deal with diseases. However, the more common problems a hobbyist and breeder would be most likely to encounter should be mentioned briefly.

Lovebirds are hardy birds which have few problems if cared for and fed properly. Even difficult species, once acclimated, prove strong if not exposed to unfavorable conditions. Exposure to disease, a drop in temperature, malnutrition or any other stressful situation can endanger the health of adult lovebirds. This can be especially sad if illness strikes a member of a proven pair.

1

(1 and 2) Lovebirds are active, bright-eyed, colorful birds, and they are in general very easy to care for. Every aviculturist should know the birds being kept and should note any and all changes in the behavior and conditions of the birds. With careful attention your birds should remain in good health for many years.

2→

Sick birds should be isolated immediately to insure that the illness will not spread to other birds in the surrounding area.

It is not difficult to tell if a bird is ill. Most sick birds will puff up and look wilted. They become lethargic and listless. They will stop eating. Sometimes running nostrils and diarrhea indicate that a bird is not well. Treatment and care must begin immediately if the bird is to survive.

Heat is one of the necessary factors in treating sick birds. When a bird becomes ill, it needs a constant high temperature of 90 degrees. The heat source can be a light bulb which can produce a sufficient quantity of heat. Test it first however, since too much or too little heat will surely kill the bird. Place it on one side of the cage so the bird can move toward or away from it, depending on its needs. Heat treatment is so effective that even an eggbound hen will slowly release her egg when kept in heat. Never turn the bulb off at night or even if the bird looks uncomfortable. The change in temperature would be too drastic. After a bird is out of danger and recuperating satisfactorily, a smaller bulb can be used until the bird is acclimated to regular room temperature.

A sick bird must be kept nourished or it will lose weight rapidly and die. It will quickly use up its body tissue and fluid in trying to maintain a normal body temperature. Encourage the bird to eat. Tempt it with all of its favorite foods. Be sure that the bird still receives its daily dose of vitamins.

Consumption of food, droppings, and the general appearance of the bird should be closely observed. The use of heat and vitamins should facilitate recovery; however, if it becomes apparent that the bird is not improving, contact a veterinarian who has knowledge and experience in treating birds. Usually a pet shop owner or an aviculturist can recommend a veterinarian. It is a good idea to have his number handy. Emergencies sometimes happen on weekends or in the middle of the night.

If medication is prescribed for the bird, use it according to the doctor's directions. Do not discontinue its use prematurely to avoid a recurrence of the illness.

Lighting is important in maintaining a bird's health as well as aiding in its recovery. The light should be fluorescent since this is closest to natural sunlight. Vita Lite with the tube spiraled or twisted provides effective lighting. In some species of parrots a lack of sunlight (vitamin A) can in itself cause various diseases.

Often illness is brought into an aviary by a new bird. Even if a bird is purchased from a reputable dealer or breeder, it should be quarantined for at least thirty days and watched closely. The bird should be kept in a separate room since some diseases are transmitted through the air. It should have its own feed and water dish, and these should not come in contact with any of those belonging to the other birds. Never dip the feed dish into the seeds; rather, pour the seeds from the bag into the dish. Also wash hands thoroughly after handling a new bird. Pacheco's parrot disease is transmitted through contact, and this is a very deadly disease. Prevention and precaution are key words in maintaining birds for breeding.

The following are several problems and diseases the breeder might encounter while maintaining an aviary.

EGGBOUND HEN

This is a situation in which the bird is incapable of laying its egg. It is puffed up, panting and trying to expel the egg. This problem is believed to be caused by a lack of proper nutrition, young age, too much weight, not enough room for flight, or a malformed egg. The best cure is to place the bird in an area where the temperature can be maintained at 90 degrees. In most cases the bird will expel the egg when placed in heat. Care should be taken when handling the bird that the egg is not ruptured. This could prove fatal.

(1) This is an unusual modification of the peach-faced lovebird. (2) This female Madagascar lovebird is easy to distinguish from the male of the species because the female lacks the gray coloring of the head. (3) This is the blue masked lovebird, a mutation of the black-masked.

2   3

Often placing several drops of cod liver oil or wheat germ oil in the bird's mouth or vent can facilitate the laying of the egg.

NAILS AND BEAKS

Overgrown beaks and nails are common in parrots, especially older ones. The nails can easily be cut back using a pair of nail clippers or scissors until the desired length is reached. A small piece is first removed and then slowly a bit more. The edges should be smoothed with a file. If bleeding occurs, the use of an antiseptic powder is recommended. Overgrown beaks can be remedied by providing sufficient chewing material for the lovebird.

GOING LIGHT

Going light is a term which signifies that the bird is losing weight and that there is a serious problem. Before purchasing, it is best to check a bird for good health. The chest should be examined to be sure it is plump and round with no bones protruding. The breastbone should have plenty of substance. The eyes and nostrils should look clean and clear, not inflamed or swollen. The foot should have most or all of its toes and nails. The bird should sit with one foot tucked in when sleeping. Sitting on both feet indicates that the bird is weak (except in the case of chicks and young birds which sometimes sleep on both feet). The body of the lovebird should have lush, healthy-looking feathers and no bald spots. Clipped wings, broken tails, or slightly picked heads are not unusual in parrot-type birds and should not be considered as undesirable. A bird which looks undernourished should not be purchased as a pet or for breeding since it is probable that illness is an underlying factor.

If the breeder observes that the lovebird is going light, it is best to place it in a heated spot and contact a veterinarian. Isolate the bird to insure the safety of other birds.

DEAD IN THE SHELL

This situation is common in lovebirds. It is caused by a deficiency in the hen's diet or the lack of humidity. The chick dies in the process of development or before being hatched. Dead in the shell also occurs occasionally in hens which have just started breeding.

STRADDLE LEGS

When a hen sits very tight on her chicks, her chicks' legs sometimes spread apart. This problem can be rectified by tying the legs together with knitting yarn. In three weeks the legs should heal together. It is a good idea to leave infertile eggs with the hen to equalize the pressure while sitting.

BROKEN BONES

Although broken bones are not common in birds, they sometimes occur. Most fractures involve wings, feet or toes. Toes are usually injured by getting the nails caught in the wire of the cage. The bird will try not to move the injured part of its body. It will take several weeks for the damage to heal. In the meantime it is best to separate the bird from others and place its feeding and water dishes nearby so the bird will not have to climb. A veterinarian sometimes will splint the bones involved in the break; however, only if the injury is very serious need this be done.

MITES

There are two types of mites that affect birds: the leg mite and the red mite. The leg mite causes scales to become extended on the leg. In some parrot-type birds these mites will grow around the beak, cere or mouth. Preparations made especially for the treatment of mites are readily available. Vaseline is also helpful in alleviating the problem.

1

(1) Feather picking in parrots is common. When a chick shows this condition, the parents are the culprits. After the chick is separated from its parents, it will quickly feather out. (2) Overgrown nails should be clipped. Great care must be taken, however, that the blood vessel which runs through part of each nail is not cut.

2→

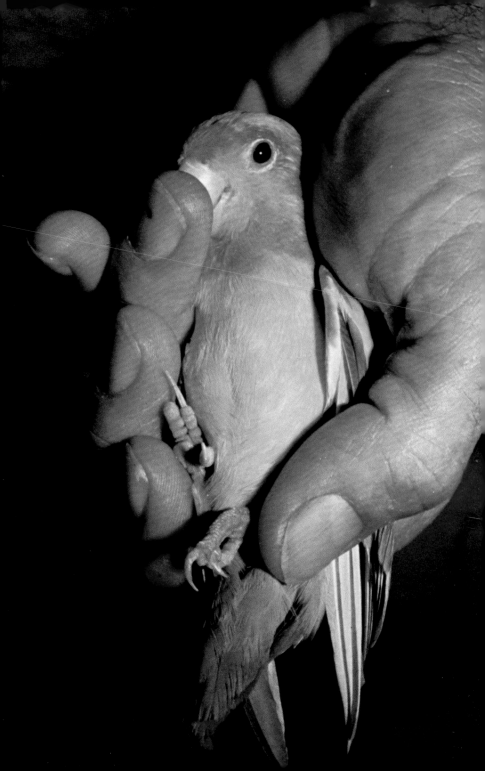

Red mites can do more damage to birds, in some cases even causing death to the chicks by sucking the blood. Since mites conceal themselves well, it can be difficult to detect them. By placing a white sheet in and around the cage at night, the mites are easily seen if they are present. They will appear as small red dots on the sheet.

Once established the red mites can be difficult to destroy. All the cages, supplies and birds should be sprayed with a solution prepared specifically to eliminate the mites. Follow the directions on the medication. New birds should also be sprayed upon entering the aviary. It is to the breeder's advantage to spray the aviary once a month to insure that the birds or cages do not harbor mites.

DIARRHEA

Diarrhea is a symptom which warns the aviculturist that an underlying illness exists. The droppings become very loose and can vary in color from white (urine) to black. Some have a foul odor. Green with white droppings are normal. If not checked, the bird will begin to lose weight and become dehydrated. Often if a bird becomes nervous for various reasons, it might have a loose stool. Usually the owner can tell if this is the case and not become alarmed.

A bird with diarrhea should be separated from other birds and placed in heat. Pet Peptin, Kaopectate, or even burnt toast can help firm the stools. Do not hesitate to contact a veterinarian if the problem continues. Lovebirds have little body weight so they cannot afford to lose body fluid.

COLDS

Colds are common in parrot-type birds which have experienced an appreciable drop in temperature or a draft. The lovebird will be puffed up and stand on two feet. The nostrils become runny with a mucous discharge. Sneezing is another symptom that indicates the bird is ill. The bird will also lose its appetite.

This is the proper way to hold a lovebird when you want to examine it.

The lovebird should be placed in a heated spot and fed what it relishes most, so it will not lose its body weight. Vitamins and antibiotics should be placed in the water.

In order to avoid colds never allow the temperature of an area to drop drastically. The change must be gradual so the bird can become acclimated to the difference. Placing a bird in a draft is very detrimental to its health and perhaps the greatest killer of birds. The bird, if housed in a cage, should not be kept in front of an open window or near an outside door.

BREEDING LOVEBIRDS
KW-125